BEYOND BORDERS

The Garden in the Rock

Passing Through Customs

If you can understand the difficulty
of traversing customs
and answering questions
"Where are you from?"
"Where are you going?"
as you wait in the drizzling rain
for the train to move on,
then you can cross the railway tracks into another country.

If you can move beyond
the sensations of your skin,
the hard edges of your mind
into some wilder, dangerous terrain,
and if you can permanently break
with your old physical idea of order
to see the weaving grasses,
then you can navigate these streets
and head out into open country.

If you can move beyond
the politics of blood,
and the tyranny of signs,
and if you can break
with what you consider taste
and touch the rain as if it were your thought,
then you can move into that other country.

If you can get beyond
the idea of borders,
pass through these customs,
then you would discover
the integrity of bridges,
the originality of streams,
the fecundity of ponds,
and you would move
among the enduring mountains,
through the valley that holds countries together.

Driving to Fort Kent in a Mid-Spring Snowfall

I stand in the office of Sullivan's Esso Station:
"Now is the winter of our discontent."
Through customs and Fraser's whirling steam I drive.
How can I romanticize this snow
smothering the ground in silicon dust,
obscuring the Madawaska Masonry dragon.
We are ready for spring:
the fields laid out in long symmetrical folds.
Red tractors wait outside of barn doors;
a convoy of ducks patrols the open pond.
Mid-April, once more, I am driving through Frenchville.

I curse the whine of snow on my tires,
and turn off the International Voice.
I've had enough of these unending drives
where white fungus clings to freezing trees.
The snow falls continuously,
a sentence with no parole.
Frenchville is endless with its Rosette,
grain towers, potato factories, empty cabooses.
Snow falls as a rumour among the tombstones:
exiled Louis XVII buried in the Frenchville cemetery.
Snow falls on the mail boxes of Hector and Ulysses.

Snow falls with *les mots inconnus*
on the daily specials of roadside eateries
at the border of Frenchville.
La neige, c'est toujours comme ça
les flocons, le givre, la rivière, tout devient vert,
étrange rêve, le brouillard sur l'eau monte
et là au-delà de la rive soudainement,
à travers le brouillard, les vieilles maisons fermées
comme les châteaux qui s'éteignent dans la brume,
se retirent comme un langage
dans l'étincelle des yeux, la lumière de l'histoire,
le temps passe, la langue, longtemps, long time ago.

Suddenly, the river breathes a green light
mammoth icebergs piled high in pantheon ruins
along the banks *et la neige continue,*
l'éblouissement des flocons.
Out along the grand prix raceway, I sing
la vitesse du présent: l'autre langue, les mots connus
et les rythmes subtils de la langue,
les champs nus, doux brillent dans la lumière,
les sons sont différents et je commence à chanter
dans les étranges mers de flocons, et toutes
les choses deviennent métaphore et flottent
dans la rivière de l'imagination.
Ici il y a le rythme de l'auto,
le rythme du piano,
le rythme du chemin
qui suit les champs, les collines
et suit une certaine distance de la rivière...

C'est la langue des ancêtres du Maine.
C'est comme un rêve, ces mots étranges
qui chantent comme les flocons.
Then ahead "Welcome to Historic Fort Kent"
The Blockhouse, Sportman's Paradise, The Optimist Club.
The spell of the snow is over.
I enter the town humming
the bars of a song from Île d'Orléans...
Quarante-deux milles de choses tranquilles...

Poems at Hoagies

Not an Acadian paradise by any means,
but this August afternoon
we pore over old poems
breathing their lives,
alchemizing experience.
Paul, as you read, your voice mingles
with the rippling voice of the waitress,
the laughter of girls on holidays,
jaunty farm boys ordering sodas.
I hear your words echo through
the ruined château of the old mill,
the dusty railway station
(now the Fort Kent Historical Museum).
In Daigle's pet store, the large plumed perroquet
squawks out of his Amazonian memory.
Down the road in the Acadian paradise
Doris carries out her "lumberjack special"
bringing news of the world to the valley,
her voice as gravelly as rapids running through pebbles
(Look at the oil painting,
where seven-year-old Doris
wildly pumps water,
her face turned into the wind,
singing an Acadian *chanson*).
And you speak of your Wisconsin home, the pause
in the clearing as you see a childhood girlfriend
The German soldier mutters to ghosts in alien woods.

It is out of this exile we write our songs,
when the poem suddenly centres us
and flows out past the large windows,
opening onto the river where blurred sunlight
shimmers on wet rocks,
purple flowers gathered thickly around the glass.
We watch men on Fish River
cleanly casting their lines.

Whether we are at Hoagies or Doris's
we transform the exile
when lightning sunlight splits trees
and outside the world flows coolly.

"Would you like anything else?"
asks the waitress.
No, only this window,
the last afternoon coffee,
                              lines breaking clear.

Demolition of the Edmundston Regional Hospital

Hôtel-Dieu is now a ruined temple under cold stars,
the columned entrance, a doorway into darkness.
Yet the hospital is not quiet:
the strumming of a faint wind,
the tinkling of surgical instruments,
an orchestral suite fading into an empty operating theatre.
Was that shadow a watchman, a looter?

Pilgrims from Madawaska, Sainte-Basile and Baker Brook,
park their cars and take snapshots.
A nurse sees the flower and coffee shop like a hotel lobby.
A surgeon recalls the criticial operations:
those patients who survived and those who did not.
For a son it is a sanctuary that holds the moments
of his father breathing his last words.
For a mother it is that moment of giving birth.
A friend comes to gaze through falling dust
upon the place where he came into the world.

The generating station is as still as a docked barge.
What is that red light within?
the torch of a late night card party of interns,
or is it the watchman on his coffee break.
Walking home, I turn for a last look;
the hospital looms as a shipwreck.
Beyond the bruised bricks on the hill
trees grow new leaves.
The stars of a constellation glimmer,
a mobile circling above a crib.

The Garden in the Rock

Slowly the garden has grown,
and so has the rock.
This year, I clear weeds from its slopes
and see how roughly-hewn it is,
how fine the layered schist.
On its terraces, my son plants portulaca
and red, shade-tolerant, impatiens.
I clear the rock around the raspberry bush
finding subtle shades of colour,
uncovering dried lichen,
feeling the rock's form as my skin.
I am changed by this rock;
geography is what I touch in my garden
where I hold the rock and sculpt with a trowel.

At the Edge of the Forest

Wind blows the leaves off the trees
among the grey trunks of the forest—
nothing to see at this time of year
before the snow comes.
As I reach the edge of the forest
I see a splash of pink.
Of course, to see the forest
I must get down on my knees
and feel the plants and the rocks.
Bending closer, I observe the pink nodules,
pick up one between my fingertips:
it is a matchstick with a pink head,
almost too tiny to handle.
All around are hundreds of lanterns lit
on this overcast October afternoon.
I study the coral of lichen,
jagged strawberry-red leaves,
moss that borders the rocks,
a cluster of star-needled spruce,
trunks turned into miniature trees
arranged as a garden in a Basho poem.
What do you call those Japanese trees?
Not until I am in my Honda,
turning the ignition
do I cry out,
                    Bonsai!

La Roche du Calvaire

In the meadow the morning is still.
The path leads to the summit of *Le Calvaire*—
no prospect of the city;
only a mowed plateau and a squat brown building
locked up with a rusted steel chain,
distant insistent drops of water,
a voice trapped in a well.

I walk until the path becomes a track,
a circular pattern of thought within my brain.
Among these cold grey stones—no skulls,
everything is in ruins: the trunks of trees ripped
from the earth in a jangled ganglia of roots;
wire torn from strewn concrete blocks,
a foundation buried under parched grass.
The forest walls me in.

Bending to the earth,
I pick up a piece of the base rock.
It is as difficult to break
as a blackboard slate.
I take another piece,
carve in a clear white arc,
draw the mountain's shape,
then scrape my own initials.

I see the shoreline contours in the rock
breaking in waves beneath the face of the earth,
the *roche mère* hidden under dirt and surface stones.
The earth is not a floor at all:
its runnels are worn from the rain.
On these moist stones I carefully walk
as they conform to my running shoes.

And—the stones—look closely
purple quartz, grey-green gneiss, rusty granite,
the shapes of flowers in the stems of stones,
igneous rock forged by ancient fire.
There, the leaves' veil is rent by a chink of light;
beyond the forest is the city.

Is it important why this place is named *Le Calvaire*?
The mind makes the mountain what it is to be.
Beyond the track at the farthest edge,
the remains of a car and a pair of workman's gloves.
Here, lovers concealed from the city,
scattered hazelnuts shells upon the ground.

Lac Temiscouata

I The Lake

On the ridge, I stopped to watch
a wave of cold white light move on the water.
I wanted to go into the woods,
but that late September day
the water called to us.
And so we took the canoe out on Temiscouata
where black smooth swells rose.
Something called in the dark rising and falling of water,
in the wind moving between slopes of the dark mountains.
There was danger in that wind
and in the swell and coldness of that water.
Our direction was not right
as we turned into the waves at a sharp angle.
What were we doing out on the water
today in this small canoe?
I wanted to store some warmth in my memory
that I could draw as a source on cold blizzard days.

II The Forest Path

I wanted to go into the forest as a way of going into myself,
to find something that would shine into my darkness,
an idea from a poem of Basho's I had read:
                              to understand the pine
I had to become the pine.
Trees were all around me...
                              but where was that pine?

I followed a white path,
going into the darkness that was myself,
following it as a means to a moment,
while you, forester, explained
the difference between balsam fir and pine
by picking needles from the branch,
by showing its suction and its point.
You rubbed your fingers up and down
until the needles rubbed off into your hands—
I inhaled the essence of pine.
You pointed out ones that were healthy
and the oddities of nature
when a tree knots itself
                              in order to correct a fault.

So we followed the rocks to the tower,
followed the uneven form of their waves
from some upheaval eons ago.
"This is schist, *a phylo silica.*"
It gleamed as I touched it,
and the sound itself, *philo*, love.
These rocks were *feuilles*—
tabula rasa, a prehistoric clay I could write on;
these lichens and moss, words
growing out of fissures
creating a new earth,
folded layer upon layer
                              metamorphosed.

III The Tower

I have returned to the lookout tower,
this place which has a wider vision of the afternoon.
It is difficult to be away from these elements,
the things of this earth.
I have to hear my voice—
let it go.
I think of your wife, Lin,
her face silent as stone.
I said I was looking for Basho's tree.
I wanted to be a tree.
I wanted to be in the sunlight.
She said I looked younger
and her face lit up.
For a few moments the stone melted.
I saw her children at the window.

Lin was without family or country,
cast adrift in the South China Sea.
She was going to pay respects to her dead father.
And I thought of my wife not free in this city,
not having friends, nor being free with me.
I thought of how she must have loved me
and loved our children to endure this cold.
She was going to pay her respects to her father who had died.

IV The Pine

I am looking for a tree, as Basho said to.
From this tower at the edge of Lac Temiscouata
across from the last great crouchings of the Appalachians.

Directly in front of me is a great white pine
reaching up into the sky,
but it is hard to look at:
the tree is almost one with the light.
My eyes tell me to choose another tree.
I survey birch, poplar and fir,
but return to this pine.
I must learn to look
at this tree in full sunlight.
I feel light and wind move through my limbs.
How good is the feeling of wind on my needles,
to feel growth in my needle tips,
to rise here into the great span of sky,
into the curve of the afternoon.
Here I grow, yet part of me is destroyed by frost and winds.
I am always drawn into this green source of the earth.

I see a hawk ride air currents,
and think of the hawk I treasured as a youth
at the boundary of country and city.
Here it has appeared.
It glides, knowing how to use the currents of air.
If only my own lines would glide as thought
and ride the air up and crest, then
dip down in the rhythm of freedom.

I wanted to be alone in the woods
with light worthy of my pain,
the pain in my wife.
I wanted to be alone
to experience the viewpoint of this tree,
but here on this forest tower
by a white pine glowing in September sun,
a gliding hawk surveys the lake,
shows my hunger,
among radiant stones.

V The Cave

I am alone.
At a bend in the path I climb down, stop
where a pine tree has fallen and a large rodent
has burrowed a den.
The roots have snapped from the earth
and lichens have becomes ghosts.
The pine, grown out of stone,
could not sustain itself.
I could almost climb into this hole
into this burrow of stone,
this lichen, this mould, this shaggy beard of roots,
climb under the rock down into the earth.
I follow my instinct into the den of the earth,
to touch roots that turn slowly to stone.

VI Shoreline

I go to the water's edge,
to the beginning of life,
and bend down to rub the rock against my chin.
It is wrinkled like the fissures of my face.
I love the texture of this rock
and the spray on my skin,
the blessing of the voice of water.
I love the way water engulfs me in its spray,
in its swirling and teeming around the rock,
in its greens, greys, and golds.
I remember the seacoast
where I went fishing on the rocks with my father.
I love the dark water crackling in the tide
in the valley of the mother rock,
feeding the waves,
                    feeding the limbs of the earth...

Gardening

Stirrings in sleep,
the brush of your thigh against mine,
our legs almost, but not quite, intertwined.
The mill pulses in the close dark,
merges into our rhythms of sleep,
mingles with early morning birdsong.
This afternoon, we had trimmed the dead branches
pulled the overgrown weeds
cut the parched grasses
to mark the borders of the garden.
At a distance, I worked
clipping the hedge
while you snipped the thorn bushes,
shaping their growth.
Then we stood beside one another
with our scratched, bitten arms.
At lunch, we argued about selling the house
and about whether or not we were soul mates.
That year we lived in the stone house in Dewittville
we worked in the nearby forest
each uncovering a path of stones through the trees—
so distant we could not hear each other.
Then cutting, snipping and clearing
we began to approach each other,
moving through wild undergrowth
through the variation of the forest
until we found our paths had grown together.
This morning I awake to the breathing of the grass,
to the touch of your body.

The Woman in the Picture

This painting is different:
as if something in you were waking up
after being asleep for a long time.
The picture is not only about bottles—
there is a woman there
standing before a bookcase.
The books are the colours of stones.
The woman is standing on blue and gold designs of a Mexican carpet,
relaxed, with her hand leaning on the case
almost as if it were a living thing.
Behind her, silhouettes of two lovers embrace.
Her eyes are closed. She is thinking
of the lake beyond the oval window.
She is outside standing on a shore by the lake,
waking up out of this winter landscape,
opening her fingers onto the curve of the hill.
Her thoughts are clear, relaxed, simply of the world.

"La Dentellière"

Bent over your lace,
everything in your body
draws me toward your hands;
I can feel the tension
as you pull the two strands of thread.

The way you bend is your inclination
to thread the form of fabric;
Your cheeks and hidden smile
(if it is a smile at all)
are directed to the point in the sewing of the blue cloth.

So I observe you concentrating
on the point of that pattern you make.
I feel the motion of your hands, forearms, shoulders
threading your life,
forgetting about children, family, history
weaving them through your fingers.

How Vermeer has poised your eloquent fingers,
your needle suspended in perfect tension.
I look at you in that gold and white dress;
the blue fabric is so tactile,
I could run my finger over it.
Lacemaker, you spin fabric out of yourself,
draw me into the flowers of the sun
as you float there
alive to the graceful interaction of work and life...

Your Face

It is hard to write of you without metaphor,
the way the sun shines on the level of the sea
or the way that surprise flickers in your eyes,
a concealed humility.
It is these that awaken desire—
the soft lines of your face,
the slow spread of your smile,
the dawn about to break.

There is a world of light in your face
that is about to be discovered.
It is what the light in the sky is all about,
openness as unexpected as an afternoon wind.

So hard to talk of metaphors.
Just between you and me
these naked words will have to do.

The Forest is Not a Forest

The Forest is Not a Forest

In the beginning I hated these mountains
for keeping the world out.
Now when I walk
I follow the timber-cut roadway,
and the path becomes the poem.
I see stories in the stones.
They draw me back to the timeless sea
and poplar, maple, fir, pine
speak of something in the wind.

        Then the rock suddenly rises
into ridges, step by step.
        I climb over the deposits,
read the scraping on a lost school slate:
wave, vein, thrust of fire.
And the wind billows through leaves like sails
jarring my mooring from the world,
releasing me from prison
as if something in me leaps out—
a light, an abandonment
              to fuse with this wind.
Rise on the waves of air like that raven there
and survey the landscape from above,
veering over old surveyors, lost lumber camps,
old crockery and broken axes,
frayed sheets of love letters,
and so I would skirt the wind
and rise out over the border of the river.

I step into the clearing
        among the rocks, goldenrod, and Queen Anne's lace
and in that space a task challenges me
to see the power in love
to look back and view the obstacles in the road
as the necessary things to come through.
I break the castle of art

search for an ideal
map, and find it,
        only to have it dissolved by a child's tear.

Here is a madness, a holding
onto the self, being separate
from the world. Pick up
that piece of rock there
                    and throw it down into dust...
Break the self,
            and walk only here
as if someone else
            as if I were that beech
  or that raven riding out there...
Give up this separate boundary
and learn just to be the feeling,
the flight of the raven,
        the line of the sea in the rock
or the colour slowly suffusing from the season,
the bark peeling from the birch.
Learn to uncover these things
and step out onto the edge
of that round rock where the world glimmers
dangerously in its fierce purity
and embrace the cold and the turbulence.
Here lose your name and name
horned snail, red lantern berries, shadowy fragrant ferns.

Walk now on the path,
as if the stones were allegories
of a life that is not yours.
Discover it as you go on
in this lightness of the falling rain
where the sky touches your forehead,
and you feel the dreams of the dog.
Go ahead—
say it isn't so:
        the forest is not a forest.

Tell us how to dream.
Why do we keep to these skins
when the lovers know how to grow beyond themselves
and slowly become one in hand and thigh?
Slowly the form assumes the world
—this is the new geography of the heart.

Riding the SMT Down the Appalachian Route on a Late October Afternoon

Already the roofs of the houses here are covered in snow,
yet as we head south it begins to disappear.
Rocks shine on exposed gravel beds,
mountain slopes extended to the river.
Synclines and geosynclines
don't follow the highway's irregular course.
Here are the Appalachians,
distant humped mountains gathered together.
How small is our presence on their slopes:
houses hugging the hillsides,
pumpkins grinning from sagging porches,
porcelain dolls for sale at a swamp's edge,
a slogan for the politician who saved the country—
even the longest covered bridge in the world.
This is how we measure human things:
the highway winding through hazy hills,
a thin band of history.

The gorges cut through the mountain
take us back to a time before billboards.
The landscape is a long-playing movie;
on the horizon the sunlight projects
its blue beams onto the furrows of farmers' fields
which follow the larger form of the hills.

Now, gradually it's getting dark.
I'm falling into sleep
to the music of the humming tires,
the percussion of the wind against the window frame.
I'm gazing into the reflection of the afternoon
riding into the mountain ridge, not following
the lines of the road
but the rock, as we enter the forest.
The wild weaving birch lean
together in a slender dance

and the hesitant tamarack are poised as filigrees;
the poplars turn and shimmer in the music.
We move through the woods following
the banks, hills, dips, and we rise
to meet the dark folds—
rise up into the wild
and down into the gorge.
Still we follow the ridge flowing
past us as if we were suspended—
and it is travelling through us.
Are we still in this moment of the music
and turning leaves and moving ridges,
moving back through the rhythm of the rocks?

The ridge suddenly falls
into the great wide forms of sandpits,
multiple planes where men are digging, with diesel shovels,
thick layers of sand and gravel. Slowly
they hollow out glacial deposits, sands the sea
deposited, over thousands of years, thousands of years ago—
how small the men are, carving out the walls,
as if they're working on a pyramid.
The bus glides down a hill along the Saint John
until there is no road,
                    only water on both sides drifting by...

We enter the outskirts of the city
past the old barns and the reformatory school,
the first mansions and busy gas stations.
The signs of hotels magnify our importance
and we forget the long distances,
                    the ancient backgrounds.

Shortcut Through the Renous

Even before we came to New Brunswick
the mover had spoken of its curves and twists,
"impossible to drive in winter."
One October we tried driving it—
vans and cars loading at the gas station
reminded me of Conrad's mouth of the Congo.
Turbulent clouds gathered
and ten minutes in
winter swept over us,
blurring the curves,
blinding the road.

Today, it's clear.
I will drive
this road across the center of New Brunswick.
Ahead, I see two men talking by their 4x4's,
recall a newscast murder
and a maximum security prison along the Renous.
A bald man in a leather jacket carries a bag.
Why is he walking alone?
I ride these curves and steep hills,
easier to negotiate in the light
past the graveyard of clear-cut forest.

Already I can see a green halo of growth—
the beginning chlorophyll, a purplish breath
announcing leaves, birches shedding
scrolls of skin-tinted bark.
Drive over the hill, the black
open stream. Put on the brakes. Stop.
Outside, sounds are everywhere.
The snow is protean
as molecular bonds break, ice rising
in the wavering steam.
A splash in the ebony water,
the brown ribbed-bottom ripples,

a slithering of mud things.
Trout swim below phosphorescent ceilings of ice.
Slime speckles the ice, a green cauliflower.
On this bridge's edge, a board
is exposed, the faded texture of an old railway tie.
I need this spring:
this dark inlet is a door.
Learn to let go
of the heart's driftwood.
Listen, the voices of clarity—
blue jays, orioles.

The bald man in the leather coat is not a convict.
It's fear on this deserted road
which makes me prisoner.
But here by the bridge, clear brown water
flows through the melting ice,
through the fissure of winter
from a deep, quiet opening.

The Gorge

We pass over the black turmoil of water,
the churning of turbines.
The waters thunder under Grand Falls.
Six years it took to tunnel through this rock.
The launch's engine splutters
as geographers eat their lunches quietly
and study these high cliffs.
Here the French explorer would
have gazed upon these cliffs,
grandeur of the New World.

Slowly we turn into the silence of the gorge
where and a cormorant skirrs over dark water.
After examining railways, lumber yards, bridges
we enter the rugged Ordovician age,
black river winding among these rocks
as it has for millions of years.
"That small stream over there," a geographer says,
"caused more erosion than this large river."

Here on the bas-relief of these rocks
are scrolled parabolas of mediaeval domes, cupolas,
and flying buttresses
carved out of a cliff.
Imagine their genesis, the veins
ribboned in chalk, fire creating an action painting
for the ages. The lines throw us
back to the forging of minerals.

Passing through this prehistoric canyon
we feel so transient.
Our captain holds his hand above his heart,
fears another cardiac arrest—
luckily, no rambunctious children on this trip.
He names the rocks:

"The Camel's Back"
    "Indian Head"
        "The Sphinx"
            "The Pulpit Rock"—
the ledge where a moose
leaped from a hunter's headlamps to its death.

These rocks could be the Giant's Causeway in Antrim,
blocks carved by great forces,
Peruvian mountain crags
where Inca temples rise into mist—
but, we are unquestionably here
gliding through the dark water,
hearing the voice of the rocks.
Water swirls through whirlpools
and their gravelly voices mingle with our own.
Here, the Saint John is so narrow,
I can almost touch both shores,
the gorge walls, with my hands.

I ask questions about the identity of rocks,
the chemical structure of the rock,
the origin and processes of geomorphology.
"Those are veins of quartz within schist," says the geographer.

I want this gorge to be inviolable,
separate from the human, as natural
as the eagle's flight;
I want its geology to be invulnerable
in its immaculate, enduring forms,
untouchable as the myth of Malobinah,
the woman who sacrificed herself for her tribe,
or the 19th century funambulist
who crossed above the thundering falls—
you can still see the spikes of the tightrope
lodged in the jagged ledge of the cliff.
I want to separate the rock from the human,
to see its powerful continuing forms.

Only last summer a young girl challenged
the gorge's face, climbed to the edge of the cliff
and almost reached the summit
when she slipped through her companion's arms
to her death below.
In the expansive reaches of this place
two birches at the lip of the canyon
quiver at the very edge of the earth.

Mountain Garden

for Audrey Côté St-Onge

Sitting on your porch I look up to terraced gardens
where tulips and daffodils waver in a windy chorus.
A path meanders up among the outcroppings
to the last flower bed.
There was nothing here
until you planted flowers and built walls,
shaping the garden as an amphitheatre.

Inside your house are paintings:
your daughter's canvas of a field of dancing wheat,
blown about like the waves on Fundy,
        your painting of childhood fields,
the farm at Rivière Verte—
          strawberries rising to defy the gravity of time.
In your studio, a still life:
a green opaque bottle
holds a lush red poppy
        against a green-yellow background—
golden brown sunflowers drying
so that they rise off the page,
dials of thick bronze mandalas.

On the easel in your studio
is a painting of birches.
Trying to get the atmosphere right
you erase textures of sky.
You etch the rocks in your garden.
Look, how these rocks
glisten with light in ridges,
        in scratches, in veins—
they almost smile in the light.
The moss with pink lanterns
lightens the miracle of lichens,
minutiae of living under the surface of things.

See how light grows out of the darkness;
you rub your fingers over the texture
as the ridges of your skin,
building it up, sculpting these rocks,
texturing the lines
until they become your field.
There, the white trunks of the birches
(where there was nothing before)
you lighten the bark
until it almost fades into the form of sky.
These trees burn at the cool edge of things.
You follow the precise eye's edge,
cutting the ridges with a trowel
out of the rock
where the birches stream upward
into the smoky-blue lines of twilight.

The Forgotten City

I

Where is your centre?
So much of your architecture has disappeared.
We try to find your history,
hold these photos up to the light of the present.
If we look beyond the birches
we can see the mill,
the smoky heart of the city.
In front of us, on a cairn, the founders,
their green stern faces molded in bronze.
Day and night transport trailers bring in their cargos of trees
and the plant pours smoke into the air.
If we read the street names,
we find politicians—no women, artists, musicians.
Across the dark oily surface of the Madawaska River,
the streets of workers remembered only by numbers.
Where we stand was once known as the *quartier anglais*.

II

Here Leonide Gagnier ran his mill:
the whirring of the saw blades,
the running of the water,
the turning of the waterwheel,
his horse looking up with sober eyes,
sniffing morning bread from the local bakery.
Later, the pungent smell of distilled whiskey
wafts up from the lower streets of *Le Bagosse*.
During Prohibition, contraband whiskey
from Europe and Saint-Pierre et Miquelon
was smuggled by night from houses through tunnels
to the bank of the Saint John River
and ferried across to Maine.

In the Sixties, Conway Academy was demolished.
Developers said it was deteriorating;
it took three bulldozers weeks to wreck it.
Across the road, The Capitol and The Star movie theatres
had enticed teenagers. Gert Michaud recalled
nuns lecturing them on sinful movies:
"We were back for the next Saturday matinee."
At the corner of Église and Canada Road
stood the old post office with its tower
overlooking the town and the Hôtel Royal
torched not long ago by an arsonist.

III

We are looking for the Maliseet cemetery,
when through the swirling dust and turbid sunshine,
an older man arrives like a *Deus ex machina*,
limping, his smile slightly askew.
"I know where the Indian cemetery is.
Conway Academy came to here," he points.
"Five yards away was Dr. Pichette's house."
We imagine the house where the library now stands,
built over the Indian graveyard.

IV

We now begin the descent toward the falls, *le petit sault,*
past the electric generating plant, away from the traffic.
On the promontory, overlooking the two rivers,
the British built a fort against the invasion of the Americans.

We look at a photo taken in 1890
when Victoria Street ran through here.
It is so detailed that we can almost step into it
and follow the Temiscouata line
to its junction with the CPR
at the end of the century.
This is a holiday
as gentlemen dressed in top hats
and ladies in long gowns sporting parasols
are strolling on the boardwalk.
There is also a clown with a mediaeval pointed hat
and children riding bikes and chasing a hoop.
Above a house a blurred flag is flying.
If you follow this road, it will bring you
to the Madawaska Inn and the Grand Hotel.

As I scan the elegant row of houses in this photo
can I find one that remains?
I look at the one with the tower,
but Marie Noelle says, "That's not it."
I look closer at the three window frames,
zoom in on that one arched window
and examine the tower—
a tower that has not changed in a hundred years.
Now, the house is a place of food and clothes for charity.
This was the centre: the hotels, the dry goods store, the drugstore,
the junction of the Temiscouata and the CPR.
(I had watched them tear up the tracks.)
The scarlet pagoda of the railway station still stands
under the grey gothic stare of Collège Saint-Louis-Maillet.

La Roche du Diable

I

For years I've heard the legend of the rock.
Conrad leads the way,
followed by my former student, Mark.
The descent is steep, the path
overgrown with thorny raspberry branches
that whip toward my face.
"Not like the old days," Conrad says,
"when the tourists came and religion was important."
The stepped ties are tilted and so slippery
I almost stumble into the undergrowth. The path
ends and I push the last branch out,

step into the clearing.
The steep river banks are separate from the forest.
I'm on the undulating Devil's Rock—
at my feet, the marks I've waited years to see:
the hoof, the hole and the gash. I hesitate
before putting my finger into the hole.
Feel warm sand and pebbles
and the rough texture of the scrape.
It's as if the mark
has been burned by the heat from a blowtorch.

II

Conrad, his arms akimbo, stares out over the rock,
tells me the story his grandmother told him.
A long time ago at the beginning of the colony
when both sides of the river was Madawaska,
when there weren't many schools,
there was a bunch of bad boys who drank, made trouble,
and broke the rules of the community.
There was one fellow worse than all of the others,
un bon vivant. *One day he unexpectedly died.*
The community didn't want him to be buried
in the new graveyard,
but since he was part of the parish
the priest decided to bury him
out of the way in the corner of the cemetery.
Well, three nights later
a local man woke up
and walked down to the river to take his nightly leak,
but right in the middle of taking a piss, he froze.
There, ahead of him
coming out of the grave was a red light
that slowly grew into the ball of a fire,
and then into a fiend with a fiery stick.
The onlooker couldn't believe his eyes.
He watched the bluish shape drift over the earth,
slide down the bank, and
scorching the rock with its hoof,
slip into the dark water.
In the morning, the man returned and saw
the scorched mark of the hoof
where the devil slid, hissed,
                    and disappeared into the river.

III

There is no devil here.
The stones are
staggered.
Ripples form around them,
yet there is a slow stirring of the water,
something uneasy in the air.
I hear hunger in the hoarse crow's cawing.
In my boots I step slowly off the rock.
Minnows dart dizzily here and there.
I pick up withered tentacles,
the crumpled body of a crab.
Over my boots leeches swim.
By the rock's edge
I see an orange-striped snake.
No, it is too immobile—
I reach into the heavy water and pick it up:
only a twisted, rusted hook—
even a human implement seems inhuman.
Everything I cup out of the water is decaying.
To the side of the rock is an old millstone.
"I've never seen that before," says Mark.
Water ripples from the millstone,
the drawing of an undertow.
The current gurgles hypnotic sounds
as if inviting me into their depths.
But I stop.

There is no order to my experience here,
only the disorder that I bring.
As I try to climb out of the river
I slip, and Mark must reach out to help me up.
We are standing at the edge looking upriver
when a squadron of gulls flies low—
dive bombers letting go of their loads,
droppings exploding onto the water.

IV

Two people drowned here, says Conrad,
Azzie was sitting here with his girlfriend picnicking
and after lunch he said he would swim across
the river to the American side.
He was an excellent swimmer
but he never made it to the other bank.
Halfway across he got a cramp
—Conrad points beyond the ripples in the river—
went under and drowned.
And his girlfriend could do nothing.

There was an old bachelor who used to come here
and sit on the rock.
He didn't bother with anybody.
People said they saw him here
just before he disappeared.
When they searched beyond Devil's Rock
they found him lying face down.

V

Why am I drawn here
to marks on these rough layers?
I read the rock's complexion,
the lines of a Rorschach stain.
I must detach myself from
the dark spirits of the river.

The arrow of the sharp rock projects into the water
So I stand and look up
into the hot afternoon.
Was that a falcon
breaking through shadow into sunlight?

Inside the Oldest House in Madawaska

Dark outlines are visible through a dusty chapel window:
a butter churn, a cedar chest, a spinning wheel.
Beside the door are the names of thirteen families
who journeyed from Sainte-Anne in 1785.
The bicentennial numbers are capped with silver flames.

Into Alexander Cyr's house, we step.
Conrad shows me the original walls
he cut down from an old house, dragging
them from the path of a bulldozer.
He cross-cut these corners, and now points
to how the house was constructed:
wooden pins holding the great planks together.
He shows me the roof he saved,
how the pioneers made shingles
using nails spaced eight inches apart.
Weighing his words carefully,
he speaks of how his ancestors cut the boards
with the rough grain of the circular saw,
and earlier, planks with the grain of a watermill.

This museum is his house.
He brings each piece to the eye,
knowing that it had been touched by his ancestors,
that the wood had felt their hands' skill.
They had shaped the sleek
curves of the birch bark canoe,
strong as the muscles in their forearms.
On the wall is a rust-stained print:
the Acadians leaving their homes
for the ships to take them into exile.

Outside, walking toward the cemetery gate,
I ask "Where are the original settlers buried?
"We don't know," says Conrad,
"The CPR came through here with the railway.

This road we're walking on was the tracks.
They found the bones of the first families
and threw them into one big hole."
His left hand is about to venture a guess, but declines.
Mark speaks up:
"We're walking on them now."

La Fenêtre

Il y a des après-midi
où le givre fait des formes
comme les mythes de l'orfèvre
les symboles sculptent en glace
les dauphins, les châteaux
les graines comme le sable
l'écume éclate,
les étoiles scintillent,
la forme d'écriture,
les lettres de Stendhal.

Il y a des soirées comme celle-ci
plus calmes, presque chaudes
quand la rivière respire le brouillard,
et obscurcit les contours précis de pays différents,
et soudainement la brume coule
sur la Roche du Calvaire comme un volcan
on pense à votre père, le raconteur
qui fait des contes de fées
sur une île dans les Caraïbes.

Et doucement, la nuit vient
et les lanternes apparaissent
comme les bijoux d'une guirlande
sur les courbes du pont
et scintillent comme les étoiles.
Elle obscurcit le miroir de la Madawaska
(on oublie la fumée du moulin Fraser)
et dans cet encadrement
votre fenêtre devient une carte postale
avec les lettres écrites en or
comme l'atmosphère douce
Edmundston by night
et les mots suspendent la nuit
dans cette étrange saison hivernale.

Le Monde-de-Stone

Edmundston, on pense changer le nom de cette ville
à Champlain ou Madawaska,
mais il existe un Madawaska à travers la frontière.
Le nom est déjà l'histoire
qui est gravée dans le cœur des habitants.
La ville a été nommée d'après le gouverneur Edmund Head
ou sa femme qui a visité la région quelque après-midi de 1852.
Maintenant le nom n'est plus anglais,
mais transformé dans un autre monde,
il a assumé la géographie des montagnes de cette ville.
Pourquoi changer le nom de cet espace dans les montagnes?

Le nom s'est inscrit dans les montagnes.
Il faut nommer les espaces de pierre;
la montagne qui monte au-delà des chemins de fer du CN,
la Roche du Calvaire, c'est l'endroit pour des amours.
Au-delà du Madawaska, c'est les montagnes qui s'allongent,
sept montagnes qui ondulent comme les corps.
De l'autre côté, il y a une montagne le sentier du Prospecteur, et
où le vieux mineur, Bob Le Bœuf, cherchait de l'or.
Il ressemble à Abraham Lincoln, mais avec une mauvaise mine.
À l'arrière du Supervalu, il n'a pas découvert l'or,
mais l'eau qui brille comme une fontaine au clair de lune.
Là, le professeur d'anglais, quand il était étudiant,
écrivit son nom dans une bouteille et nomma sa montagne.

L'histoire s'est écrite dans la roche.
Quand je suis arrivé ici, je suis entré dans le "collège"
et j'ai vu les grandes toiles: la déportation des Acadiens
et le commencement du grand dérangement.
On voit les familles se préparer pour embarquer vers l'exil,
mais l'année scolaire suivante, les toiles ont disparu,
remplacées par une machine à Pepsi.

Ici, l'hiver est long, l'hiver est dur.
Tout devient froid
et la glace et le gel transforment les pays en pierre.
La neige crée une sorte d'oubli;
il y a des matins où on oublie les choses,
comme un moment gelé dans le temps.

Et je suis debout dans un couloir
et le moment est gelé
dans le temps oublié;
le moment en Amérique
quand la mère avec sa caméra
dit à sa fille,
"Fromage."
"*What's fromage?*"
"*Smile!*"

C'est le moment où
Léopold Lang, dans un couloir de fenêtres,
a levé la main vers l'Amérique et dit,
"Autrefois, c'était à nous."

Où est cet espace?
Quand les étrangers arrivent ici,
ils ne savent plus:
quelles montagnes, quels bâtiments
sont au Canada et lesquels sont aux États-Unis?
Qu'est-ce que cette république,
cette république mythique,
qui a emprunté son drapeau
avec ses étoiles rouges et l'aigle.
Et après le conflit des frontières
le Colonel fut exilé à Baker Brook.
On n'a pas besoin d'étoiles de peuples.
Voyez, le pub Costigan
où les lumières brillent sur les tombes anglaises.
Costigan, un homme qui a prévenu la violence
entre les Français et les Anglais.

Avez-vous quelque chose à déclarer...
Non, je ne déclare rien,
mais il existe la langue
la langue dure dans cette histoire.
Je me souviens d'un matin
marchant au sommet du Calvaire,
et je cherche des fleurs à Saint-Basile;
ici, c'est le berceau, le cimetière,
et les chemins de croix,
et le chemin de fer,
et l'espace des familles fondatrices;
on voit leur nom en pierres.
Ici on voit les pierres dans l'herbe
et la lumière qui brille sur le chemin de fer,
et sur la petite chapelle avec les artefacts
et sur les courants qui entourent la Roche du Diable.

Et dans les jardins de Picver,
Jean-Pierre m'a montré une toile qu'il a peinte
des premiers pionniers:
le fleuve, les bancs, la végétation.
C'est l'origine de ses ancêtres sur cette carte.
C'est le premier hiver de faim
et d'isolement dans la neige.
Maintenant il marche parmi les pins et la pente de fleurs,
et il lève une pierre grise,
et il me montre les fleurs fossilisées dans la roche
comme une écriture sur le tableau noir de la Terre.

Anniversaries

Aunt Cornelia

Of course, you went by other names:
Corrie, Connie and *Tante Cockie*.
Christmas mornings, you owned the bathroom on Habitant Drive,
emerging two hours later as Queen Nefertiti,
your gleaming body wrapped in a CP hotel towel,
hair bound in a swirling turban,
eyebrows singed into perfect *accent circonflexes*.

We heard rumours of imminent marriages—
the reporter at *The Globe and Mail* who wrestled a bear,
some wealthy businessman or other in Europe,
a millionaire cattle rancher in Texas—
but the engagements were inevitably broken.
And you would suddenly appear for a whirlwind visit
carrying souvenir towels from Mexico or Spain.

Your elocution was perfect, as if you were auditioning,
with only the faintest quiver of a Dutch accent.
You lived as a high-class model at the Royal York Hotel,
and when we visited, you had our snacks sent up by room service.
Later, in a perfumed apartment in Rosedale,
your bedroom was decorated with Venetian canals
and souvenirs of matadors in Mexico City;
above your bed, an embossed velvet legend of Hiawatha
surrounded by moist-eyed deer.

You became friends with "our pet, Juliette,"
and Rutenberg at Holt and Renfrew.
You once caught TB, which you got over,
but you never got over Canadian winters.
So you flew to California, opened a boutique
and served Doris Day and other movie stars.

Word finally reached us that you were marrying
a wealthy Hungarian engineer—the nephew of Zsa Zsa Gabor.
There was a daughter we were never to meet.
Your brother, Herman, went to visit you in Los Angeles,
had to chase your chimpanzee up a neighbour's balcony.
Later, your husband went crazy from too much drinking.
You emigrated from Santa Monica to Arizona,
the final antidote to Canada.

These are the pictures that I have of you,
but there is one I left out: Christmas Eve, 1956,
when you and mother made *ollie bollen*, laughed
and sang Dutch songs, ran
up and down the stairs, tossed
flour at each other
until it rained down,
changed you into ghost girls.

"Tear off Your Yellow Star"

"My children, Alexander and Fenna, where are you?
Look around at us
being taken away in cattle cars—
the gas chambers are not rumours.
Tomorrow we're being shipped to Westerbork
My mother and brother are already
on their way to Auschwitz.
How many of us are left?
There, by the fence, raspberries.
Ben, when was the last time you ate raspberries?
They're delicious.
I'm ripping off my yellow star."
"Gerhart, leave the star. They'll kill you."
"Not if we walk now.
The guards are down the line.
Tear off your yellow star.
Let's go for a walk."

Years later, he remembered that night:
Ben and he walking on the edge of the gravel,
away from the death camp,
walking in the direction of the *Zuiderzee*
until his shoes grew ragged
until darkness erased his path.

Refuge in Friesland

Fenna won't go to see *Schindler's List*;
few of her relatives escaped.
Tante Rose forged her passport,
taught piano lessons all of her life in New York City.
Her grandmother and uncles were gased in Auschwitz.
Her father escaped before being sent to Westerbork.
I hold a negative plate up to the light,
see the ghostly figures of her family.

Some Jewish people sent their children to Friesland.
There wasn't enough to eat;
Fanna scrounged bulbs in outlying fields,
swallowing their bitter juice.
When she became as thin as a rake,
her mother said they had to escape.
so one night, through a biting mist,
their boat crept out into the *Zuiderzee*.
Machine gun bullets ricocheted off the hull
as smuggled children crouched under potato sacks,
waiting in the uneasy silence
until the sun broke on the Friesland shore.

At the marketplace,
farmers chose the children they wanted.
"I like this one."
"No, this one."
"This one is healthy."
At the end, only two children stood on the platform—
Alexander and Fenna,
who wouldn't leave without her brother.
One farmer agreed to take both of them.

Foraging

Uncle Herman speaks through his steaming coffee,
"I could've killed the foreman today. He told me
'Veldhuisen, put your back into it, man.'
The sweat was pouring off me
and he was standing over me like the Gestapo.

"The spring of '45, was bleak—
you could feel fear in the land.
I had to sneak out of the house for firewood.
And I had to run quickly through the shadows—
at any moment there could be
angry officers and their questions.
They could send you to a work camp for nothing.
I stole some paintings from the gallery.
I didn't want the Nazis to get them."
His clear eyes gazed through the cigarette smoke.

"My hands were numb from the biting wind.
The ditches were muddy.
I had to jump over a fence onto the forest floor.
The wind was howling through the bare branches.
I was scared, but when it was over
my mother gave me an extra slice of bread."
His face broke into a smile.

"One morning, I was later than usual getting back.
 I was desperate as I dragged my bundle of sticks
through the deep snow.
Each time I lifted it,
I sank under the weight,
and as I tried to heave it over
a fence my knuckles bled.
I cried.
We needed that wood.

"That spring, wood was scarce
and patrols came more often.
Hauling my bundle across a field, I stopped—
a German on his motorcycle veered round the bend.
I dropped my sticks into the grass,
ran and slipped among the reeds in the pond.
The freezing water was up to my neck.
I was shivering, my teeth chattering.
Had he seen me?
Ripples spread through the water.
He looked right over my head, grunted,
got back onto his bike and roared off.

"It gets me so god-damned angry
when bastards like the foreman
act as if they own the world.
I took my shovel like a crowbar
and pinned him up against the furnace wall.
I could see the fire burning in his eyes."

Return to Wassenaar

Robert, you show me your scrapbook:
photographs of the camp, the soccer field, movie stars.
A blonde girl smiles through onionskin paper.
You quickly turn the page.

For two years you labour in the camp,
In those final days, the Bürgermeister implores the German officers
to spare the city, but they refuse and hang him.
By Christmas, 1944, Singen is captured by the French.
You cycle beyond the barbed-wire gate.
You cannot believe it:
the road ahead is the road home.
Later, you stay in the commander's villa
and find a tall statue of Hitler.
The war is still going on in Holland.

Monsieur Robert Veldhuisen et Ferdinand Linterman, de nationalité
hollandaise, désirent retourner dans leur pays natal (Hollande)
(avec des bicyclettes)
                    Pour le Gouvernement Militaire:
Le Maire
          Der Bürgermeister
          commander of the regiment.

(Ferdinand is killed in a plane crash in Lisbon, 1959.)

You reach Strasbourg and cycle on to Brussels
past the burnt-out tanks and blasted bunkers.
The army is allowing no one into Holland.
The country is in quarantine.
Oma doesn't know if you are dead or alive.
For more than ten months she hasn't heard anything.
You send a basket with candles, bread, and sugar
to the *Sandhorstlaan.*

The Germans are still fighting.
The children are starving.
You are smuggled under the
tarp of a supply truck,
and peek out
onto the broken dykes,
farmers' flooded fields.

Driving out of *D's Gravenhage,*
there is the ache of the familiar red-tiled houses:
you remember the *Sandhorstlaan*
where Oma is waiting.

Liberation

On TV, veteran Canadian soldiers in Apeldoorn
ride armoured vehicles,
handing out chocolate bars as they receive flowers
from Dutch citizens, as they did fifty years ago.
Later, cleaning the attic,
I uncover your canvas, Herman,
hold it in my outstretched hands.
You called it, "The Last Day of the War."

A fisherman stands at the edge of the canal.
Flags are blowing freely on three red-capped windmills.
In the water a pole with a crumpled swastika sinks
and a broken sign *Spergebeit,* "curfew," drifts away.

It is spring. The cows are chewing grass,
Canada geese fly in a V formation,
while seagulls throng in a bright updraft of air.
On a path, ducklings straggle after their mother.
Near the fisherman's boat a crane forages.

Everything is in motion:
the yellow-white lilies flicker among the bullrushes.
The rays of the sun break through the clouds,
fall onto the breaking waves.
By the bank the shadowy fisherman casts his rod.
His coat, cap, and even his face, are dark.

Across the water is a Dutch girl,
dressed all in black, except for her white hat.
She hangs white panties on a clothesline.
Wind blows her skirt above her knees.
She is looking at the fisherman across the water.
He is looking at the bobbing float
where a fish has taken his line under the barbed wire.
Soon, he will look up.

Wandering in Late Night Brussels

From Brussels Central Railway Station
I try to phone New Brunswick, but all of the operators are asleep.
I have French francs, Dutch guilders, Deutsche marks
but no Belgian francs.
Near midnight, the station becomes a semi-abandoned temple:
a Chinese lady searching for a phone directory,
a Dutch girl looking for a bus out of the Centrum,
two Arabic students trying to buy a ticket out of the country.

I step out into the night looking for *wisel*.
Once again I'm the stranger wandering the street,
looking for a place to sleep.
How much is a Belgian franc?
On I wander by neon-lit mediaeval churches,
past the omnivorous tourists
ferreting out the public truths of statues,
and jugglers juggling their nocturnal lives,
the money-brokers sweating behind grills,
the pickpockets moving unctuously as diplomats through crowds
as turbulent clouds interlock like lovers in a Rubens' canvas.

I walk through the marble doorway into the Palace of David—
only 2,500 francs for the night.
How much is a Belgian franc? I imagine
working months to pay for this one night.
I leave the main thoroughfare,
think of Browning's Childe Roland
as I trudge farther into the dark circular streets.
Six trains today. I could've been in Paris.

Now the signs flicker:
Phoenix   les Félines vous présentent leur show de Travestis
*   Hong Hoah   White Horse*
Barclay's   Moonlight Night Shop

The tourists have vanished;
conspirators lean in doorways, whispering.
I, who have entered the underworld,
ask an unshaven boxer in a dark suit:
"Est-ce qu'il y a un hôtel près d'ici."
His facial muscles stiffen,
"Sommeil. L'Hôtel Sommeil."

Past the *Moonlit Night Shop* I follow him
farther into these dark streets,
imagine morning headlines:
CANADIAN POET STRANGLED IN BRUSSELS' SLEEP HOTEL.
I'm too tired to find a place.
He points silently to a hotel at the end of a laneway.

Behind the counter sits Peter Lorre and his cronies.
A young night clerk from Pakistan
unfolds a map of the city,
gives the value of the Belgian franc
and invites me to visit Brussels again.

Geel War Cemetery, Belgium

At the gate, an old man with a scarred face
speaking in a language I do not understand
guides me to the registry of soldiers.
Through the pages I search for you,
great-uncle, for whom I am named.
You served in the Second British Army,
fought in the battle of the Meuse-Escaut Canal.

When I was on the phone overlooking the runway
at Pearson International Airport last year,
father told me how you climbed out of a foxhole
to drag a wounded comrade to safety,
but as you reached for him
a bullet pierced your brain.

You may have died on a day like today,
that last morning, sipping coffee
writing a letter to your wife and daughter,
recalling a furlough in Piccadilly Circus.
Already you hear gunfire
beyond the river that you would not cross.

At the end of row D, I find your gravestone
with a shamrock and "QUIS SEPARABIT
L. Hutchman, Irish Guards, 14 September, 1944."
All goes on in the world as it has before:
the church bells peel for evening service,
the rooster crows in the field,
the persistent sound of mourning doves,
purple roses grow by the barbed wire fence,
the old farmer digs up weeds in the garden,
as he did fifty years ago, under the sound of gunfire.

It is not my sadness at seeing only your grave,
but so many other graves
with the inscriptions from the Bible and the Torah,

men scarcely in their twenties.
I cannot read many of them.
I am alone. The wind is cold.

Wild Irish guardsman,
I place a purple rose under your name.
The old man is standing by the gate,
his son and daughter-in-law waiting impatiently:
he draws me a map to the Geel railway station.
He knows why I am here.

Sources of the Nile

Joyce's Door

After the racquetball game,
I sit at a kitchen table in Fort Kent, Maine.
The picture frame on the wall
reminds me of the door at 7 Eccles Street,
the day I retraced Stephen Dedalus's route
through Dublin past Dean Swift's church
out toward the Martello Tower...

An old washerwoman carrying a bucket of milk
totters up the road
                                    toward the tower.
Buck Mulligan stands on the wooden divingboard
intones *Thus Spakest Zarathustra*
before plunging into the grey celluloid sea.

Desiring to swim, I strip naked,
walk down to the bathing pool
and somersault from the divingboard
under the spinning sun.
The October sea breathes around me.
Glistening and invigorated,
I step out of the water
and climb the staggered white stones.
Three mythical old men huddle in a cave, chorusing,
"You'll be givin' this place a bad reputation."

At the National Library I asked for the original *Portrait....*
The bald, spectacled librarian said,
"You need to be working on your dissertation,"
and returned with two green volumes in a swimming basket.
That afternoon, I followed Stephen's life
through Joyce's sea-green handwriting.

At the locked gate in front of the tower
I meet a Jewish woman,
a scholar with an invalid husband in Tel Aviv;
we decide to climb the fence,
the weight of her haunches on my shoulders,
as I heave her over the black spikes,
sign on the door, *Closed for the Season.*

I leave her and walk along the railway ties,
I cradle the pink shells from Yeats's grave,
then, one by one, I pitch them into the sea.
Cast a cold eye
On life, on death.

A rainbow arches over Dublin Bay
all the way to the purple heights of Howth Head.
On the shore, I read the stones,
Signatures of all things I am here to read...
Am I walking into eternity along Sandymount Strand?

The day ends as I arrive at 7 Eccles Street.
No house—only a space between row houses.
In the framed doorway I stand
rub the rough wood grain.
Had not Joyce passed through this doorway of Byrne's house?
Had he not created life out of life?
Stephen, locked out, squeezes under the gate,
gains access to Bloom's house.
In the kitchen, Leopold and he
sip their cups of cocoa.
Upstairs, Molly, in her bed, murmurs
love's old sweet song.

It is Dublin, 1968. *Ulysses* is banned.
The constabulary has attacked the civil right's marchers,
Ian Paisley has begun his protest against Rome.
The great beast has stirred once more.
Dubliners will not keep this house.
Now there is only this pile of stones and door frame.

In this Maine kitchen
I Ifeel I am back in Mulligan's Pub
hearing the wild drumbeat.
Framed on the red wall
hangs the door from 7 Eccles Street,
its boards grained with a million meanings,
light breaking over the dark texture of Guinness.

Lighthouse

Wind tugs at the mosquito net,
and out on the bay
the moon shines coldly over Île Bonaventure;
a thousand thronging birds begin to settle for the night,
only a few stragglers gliding over the waves toward the cliffs.

The lighthouse spreads its beacon across the waters
over the years of shipwrecks and their legends.
I take a gulp of wine;
there the surge of the sea,
the moon, the island and the lighthouse,
a stage set for our separate human destinies.

This afternoon in our Datsun 510 we struggled up Gargantua,
only to find the campground full,
overheard a Rabelaisian laughter on the summit.
Now we pitch our tent in an overflow field,
warm palms over barbecue coals,
feel wind blow across waves and tall grasses.

I lift the bottle toward the stars.
It is good to be near the sea again.
I salute the constellations
and think of the journeys yet to make.
The beacon flickers over entwined lovers
and the dark bows of cargo freighters.

Take another sip and feel the warmth.
Is this not what we wanted?—
a fire, the sea, even the cold wind
awakening us to the never ending realities of space,
as we work out the patterns of our lives under the zodiac.

How good this red wine is.
Beyond us lie a white house,
The Three Sisters and Percé,
green waves rolling through its archway,
separating it from the mainland,

Here, under the shadow of Gargantua,
the earth folded from the upheaval of forces,
we gather at the edge of the continent
looking out at the slow circling light,
think of our future as we watch
the last white birds gliding toward the cliffs of Île Bonaventure.

Woman in the Dionysos

As I lift my coffee cup
a woman rises to the music,
spins through startled air.
Diners turn their heads
towards this dancing, corporeal woman.
Her hands are leaves
rippling in the wind.
She is a bellydancer gliding
among the helmets, icons and amphorae
in this cavernous room.
The waiter walks toward her,
"Sit down, please."
"No one in my life tells me to sit down."
The manager raises his fingers,
the waiter bows, crosses his heart,
"I'm sorry," he says to the other diners.
She dances toward the bouzouki player,
her arms slowly encircling him:
J'aime les Grecs.
At the end of the table
a man in a grey suit
forms his finger and thumb into a circle,
then rises, joining the woman
and they dance.

The Golden Fleece

Christina points to the map of Greece.
"You know, very wise men come to Greece
and translate the myths.
You look at what they write,
but it is wrong.
Volvos was the home of Jason and the Argonauts."
"In high school," I reply, "we read
'Jason and the Golden Fleece.'"
"What is Jason and the golden fleece?"
Christina asks, shaking her grey-blond hair.
"What is fleece?"
It's from sheep.
Fleece, a vest—this is ridiculous...
They go all the way to Colchis for a sheep's vest.
That's just a story."

"Here, I will show you where Colchis is.
A scholar makes a new *Argo*
and he sails it all around the coast."
She draws her finger along the shores on the map
following the ship through rough waters
under steep cliffs and high fortresses.

"I was born in Vólvos.
You can see the *Argo* in the harbour.
I will tell you what the golden fleece was:
it was a river of gold.
Men took fleece from sheep,"
she rumples up her tea towel like a woolly shirt,
"and they panned for gold in the river.
That's why they came all the way to Greece."

Ghost Town

Sunday is cold and dark:
wind sweeps blackboard sky over desolate water.
Children shout, dogs run after tattooed cars.
Grouard's church leans into the wind,
strong as the Bishop's fingers
that trimmed red-veined beams and drew burning hearts.
The people named the town after him.
When he died they torched his residence,
burned paintings stored in the attic.

You speak of Ghost-Pipe, who married
a crippled girl and, when she died, he searched
for her in the Land of the Dead.
The path narrows to a gate sign
where I trace worn words:

> This Place Holy Ground
> Do Not Play Here

Plastic flowers cover first graves,
no headstones, only licence plates,
a photograph of a fisherman—
his stained face an illegible map,
a boy killed in a car crash,
a lance corporal who died of a coronary,
four children in the flu epidemic of 1918.

The grass reaches our waist.
We stumble into trenches,
cannot tell grass from grave:
"Watch out, or we might find ourselves
six feet under."
Others are sailors who floundered in the tide.

Ghosts sing of the last night:
    reckless boys,
        rebellious girls,
     lonely priests,
         forgotten soldiers.

Twilight sky turns slowly into darkness.
We stand on the edge of the glassy world
where prospectors once travelled north
          along the Heart River.
Ghost-Pipe's wife returned
        to the Land of the Dead.
The Bishop's stories
      buried in the legends of these tombs.

Still, dogs run,
    bark crazily before the street's facade.
Children spin on their bicycles,
    try to elude the court nets.
Darkness ebbs over the ridge,
     over the great expanse of glowing nothing.

Jacob in Edmonton

Jacob, you smile as you stand before me,
your intelligent eyes glistening.
I see you pacing Moscow streets,
visiting a museum from an older Russia,
waving goodbye to a long time friend.
I see the place where you grew up,
walking by the stream in the grove—
all turned into grey highrises.

In class, when I asked who had seen "David,"
only you put up your hand.

You say that place is not important:
Einstein would have been Einstein
no matter where he was born.

You pace Moscow streets
taking Hebrew lessons secretly,
always fearing a knock at the door.
        You study *Hamlet*,
say there is no hope for him either.
Yet, you are here,
        on the banks of the North Saskatchewan
in this western city,
        quiet, afraid to say too much,
                even here.

Sources of the Nile

for Gamal Rushdy

Sitting on the dark porch this late August night,
listening to the constant humming of the mill,
a steamer moving along a river of darkness,
night distilling into a timeless dream,
we talk of our notions of home.

Gamal, you speak of the great days of Alexandria
when the port was a cosmopolitan city, a part of Europe.
You left Egypt with your family,
for a new life in Ethiopia,
in those heady days when Haile Selassie ruled.

Africa breathes through your words:
we could be in Timbuktu,
or one of the lost cities of Africa.
You describe journeys to the sources of the Nile.
(In *Other Lands and Peoples*,
on a white and black map,
we traced the journeys of Livingstone
into the heart of the dark continent.)
"For centuries, the Arabs had been exploring Asia and Africa
and writing books about it.

"It was not Livingstone who discovered
the Nile but a German who erected a pyramid there.
As you know, Livingstone thought
that the Nile flowed out of Lake Victoria.
But there are several sources.
There is the source of the Blue Nile.
There is the main source of the White Nile
that flows through Lake Jinja—
it is in Uganda.
There is a source in Burundi.
There is the source in the Blue Mountains of the Moon
near the place of King Solomon's mines.

Philip carries trifle through the shadows of the porch;
I taste the fullness of the moment.
An apricot, like a midnight moon, rises.
A cool kiwi slice floats as a lily pad,
tingling grapes nestle in
banks of crust and custard.

Gamal, your forehead gleams as a mountainside.
You believe in the diversity of rivers,
never beginning merely from one source.
You speak eloquently in English, French and Arabic.
Your voice flows and eddies as the river
draws from its different origins,
from hidden branches and subtle tributaries.
You speak of the history of words:
apples, paradise, spirit.
Listening to the din of the mill
I sip ginger ale—
Africa moored out there
in the dark night of Madawaska.

A Selection of Our Titles in Print

A Lad from Brantford (David Adams Richards) essays	0-921411-25-1	11.95
All the Other Phil Thompsons Are Dead (Thompson) poetry	1-896647-05-7	12.95
A View from the Bucket (Jean Redekopp) memoir, history	0-921411-52-9	14.95
bagne, or, Criteria for Heaven (rob mclennan) poetry	1-896647-32-4	15.88
Bathory (Moynan King) drama	1-896647-36-7	14.95
Best in Life (Ted Mouradian) self-help, business	0-921411-55-3	18.69
Beyond Borders (Laurence Hutchman) poetry	1-896647-25-1	13.95
CHSR Poetry Slam (Andrew Titus, ed.) poetry	1-896647-06-5	10.95
Combustible Light (Matt Santateresa) poetry	0-921411-97-9	12.95
Cover Makes a Set (Joe Blades) poetry	0-919957-60-9	8.95
Cranmer and Pole—Archbishops (Robert Hawkes) poetry	1-896647-33-2	15.88
Crossroads Cant (Grace, Seabrook, Shafiq, Shin) poetry	0-921411-48-0	13.95
Dark Seasons (Georg Trakl; Robin Skelton, trans.) poetry	0-921411-22-7	10.95
Dividing the Fire (Robert B. Richards) poetry	1-896647-15-4	4.95
Elemental Mind (K.V. Skene) poetry	1-896647-16-2	10.95
for a cappuccino on Bloor (kath macLean) poetry	0-921411-74-X	13.95
Gift of Screws (Robin Hannah) poetry	0-921411-56-1	12.95
Heart-Beat of Healing (Denise DeMoura) poetry	1-896647-27-8	4.95
Heaven of Small Moments (Allan Cooper) poetry	0-921411-79-0	12.95
Herbarium of Souls (Vladimir Tasic) short fiction	0-921411-72-3	14.95
I Hope It Don't Rain Tonight (Phillip Igloliorti) poetry	0-921411-57-X	11.95
Imprints and Casualties (Anne Burke, editor) lit. criticism	1-896647-24-3	19.63
Like Minds (Shannon Friesen) short fiction	0-921411-81-2	14.95
Manitoba highway map (rob mclennan) poetry	0-921411-89-8	13.95
Memories of Sandy Point, St. George's Bay, Newfoundland (Phyllis Pieroway) memoir, history	0-921411-33-2	14.95
New Power (Christine Lowther) poetry	0-921411-94-4	11.95
Notes on drowning (rob mclennan) poetry	0-921411-75-8	13.95
Open 24 Hours (Anne Burke, D.C. Reid, Brenda Niskala Joe Blades, rob mclennan) poetry	0-921411-64-2	13.95
Open Road West (Joe Blades) poetry	1-896647-30-8	13.95
Railway Station (karl wendt) poetry	0-921411-82-0	11.95
Reader Be Thou Also Ready (Robert James) novel	1-896647-26-X	18.69
Rum River (Raymond Fraser) short fiction	0-921411-61-8	16.95
Seeing the World with One Eye (Edward Gates) poetry	0-921411-69-3	12.95
ShadowyTechnicians: New Ottawa Poets (mclennan, ed.)	0-921411-71-5	16.95
Song of the Vulgar Starling (Eric Miller) poetry	0-921411-93-6	14.95
Speaking Through Jagged Rock (Connie Fife) poetry	0-921411-99-5	12.95
Tales for an Urban Sky (Alice Major) poetry	1-896647-11-1	13.95
The Curse of Gutenberg (Dan Daniels) short fiction	1-896647-23-5	16.95
The Longest Winter (Julie Doiron, Ian Roy) photos & fiction	0-921411-95-2	18.69
Túnel de proa verde / Tunnel of the Green Prow (Nela Rio; Hugh Hazelton, translator) poetry	0-921411-80-4	13.95
Wharves and Breakwaters of Yarmouth County, Nova Scotia (Sarah Petite) art, travel	1-896647-13-8	17.95
What Morning Illuminates (Suzanne Hancock) poetry	1-896647-18-9	4.95
What Was Always Hers (Uma Parameswaran) fiction	1-896647-12-X	17.95

www.brokenjaw.com hosts our catalogue, author events news, submissions guidelines, maunscript award competitions, tradebook sales representation, distribution and order fulfilment information. BJP eBooks of some titles are also available. Directly from us, all individual orders must be prepaid. All Canadian orders must add 7% GST/HST (Canada Customs and Revenue Agency Number: 12489 7943 RT0001).
BROKEN JAW PRESS, Box 596 Stn A, Fredericton NB E3B 5A6, Canada.